GREAT PETS

# Horses

## Gail Mack

Marshall Cavendish
Benchmark
New York

Marshall Cavendish Benchmark
99 White Plains Road
Tarrytown, New York 10591
www.marshallcavendish.us

All websites were available and accurate when this book was sent to press.

Library of Congress Cataloging-in-Publication Data
Mack, Gail.
Horses / by Gail Mack.
p. cm. -- (Great pets)
Summary: "Describes the characteristics and behavior of pet horses, also
discussing their physical appearance and place in history"--Provided by
publisher.
Includes bibliographical references and index.
ISBN 978-0-7614-4147-2
1. Horses--Juvenile literature. I. Title.
SF302.M243 2010
636.1--dc22
2008037262

Front cover: A Thoroughbred horse
Back cover: Shetland ponies

Photo research by Candlepants Incorporated
Front Cover: Alamy
The photographs in this book are used by permission and through the courtesy of:
Getty Images: 7;  Alan Thornton, 1; Robert Harding, 4; Noah Clayton, 6; The Bridgeman Art Library / French School: 9;
Clarissa Leahy, 10; Betsie Van Der Meer, 13, 30; Bob Langrish, 14, 34, 35, 41; Tariq Dajani, 15; John Kelly, 18; Kathi
Lamm, 20; JupiterImages, 29; West Rock, 32;  Mike Brinson, 38; Thomas Northcut, 39; Philip and Karen Smith, 40;
Cornelia Doerr, 42; altrendo images, 43; Jonnie Miles, 44; David Tipling, back cover. Art Resource / Erich Lessing: 8.
Alamy: Juniors Bildarchiv, 12, 16, 21, 26; Real Image, 23; Mark J. Barrett, 24; WILDLIFE GmbH, 25. Animals Animals /
Earth Scenes: Bob Langrish, 22. AP: 28.

Editor: Karen Ang
Publisher: Michelle Bisson
Art Director: Anahid Hamparian
Series Design by: Elynn Cohen

Printed in Malaysia
6 5 4 3 2 1

# Contents

# 1

# Partners and Friends

Horses and humans have lived and worked together for thousands of years. Ancient pictures of horses are scratched into the walls of caves where early humans once lived. At first, these ancient peoples probably hunted horses for food. But when they saw how fast horses could run, they learned to ride them in order to hunt other animals for food.

As people found more uses for these beautiful, powerful creatures, horses became their partners, sharing their lives and work. Horses pulled chariots for ancient Romans and Egyptians. In medieval times, huge horses carried knights into battle. Horses pulled the covered wagons of the pioneers who crossed America to settle the West. Pony Express horses helped to deliver mail. Horses pulled wagons and plows for farmers, and helped ranchers herd cattle. Long before cars and trucks were invented, horses pulled stagecoaches for travelers, carts for peddlers who sold goods, and carriages for people to ride in.

*This ancient cave painting of a horse was made more than 10,000 years ago by people who lived in the region that includes present-day France.*

*Humans and horses have been work partners for thousands of years. Throughout history, farmers and ranchers have worked with horses to manage their land and livestock.*

*Specially trained therapy horses often help people of all ages.*

Today, horses are still an important part of many people's lives. Police horses help officers protect many of our cities. Working horses still have jobs on farms and ranches, helping people herd smaller livestock, or pull heavy loads. Specially trained therapy horses work with children and adults to ease their illnesses and bring them love and joy. Race horses and show horses—and their riders—amaze and entertain us. Many horses are simply beloved companions for their riders, who enjoy their power, their beauty, and their company.

*In some ancient myths, a Greek god named Helios used a horse-drawn chariot to carry the Sun across the sky.*

## Horses in Myths and Legends

Horses appear in the myths and legends in many world cultures. Ancient Greeks thought gods and brave warriors rode these majestic creatures. In one myth, a warrior named Bellerophon rode a snow-white winged horse named Pegasus. Together they destroyed a fierce, fire-breathing monster with the head of a lion, the body of a goat, and the tail of a dragon. Bellerophon wanted to go with Pegasus up to Mount Olympus, the home of the gods. However, Zeus, who was king of the gods, did not permit this because Bellerophon was human and did not belong there. Pegasus flew up to Olympus without Bellerophon, and spent time carrying Zeus's lightning and thunderbolts. Eventually, Pegasus flew up to live among the stars. A constellation, or collection of stars, representing Pegasus can often be seen in the night sky.

In ancient times, people in many parts of the world believed in unicorns, which were animals with one long horn on their foreheads. Some unicorns were the size of goats, and others as big as horses. They often had long beards or wore bright colors. People believed that a unicorn could dip its horn into poisoned water and make it pure so that other animals could drink.

Unicorns are mythical creatures that were believed to have magical powers.

Famous or legendary horses also appear in literature, television shows, and movies. From the mysterious and handsome horses in *Black Beauty,* and *The Black Stallion,* to loyal companions, such as the horse in *My Friend Flicka* or the Lone Ranger's stallion, Silver, horses inspire great wonder. In legends, stories, and real life, horses and humans share great affection and respect for each other. They are truly partners and friends.

# 2

# Is a Horse Right for You?

**H**orses make great pets and working companions, but they are not right for everyone. You must have the space to keep the horse healthy and safe, and the money and time to spend on its needs. Careful thought is needed whenever considering any pet—especially a horse.

## Can You Afford a Horse?

When you and your family decide to own a horse as a pet, you take on a huge responsibility. Buying and keeping a horse is expensive, and keeping it healthy and happy is a big job. The price you pay for your horse is just the beginning. You will need to pay for food, grooming tools, blankets, saddles and bridles, a **farrier**—or blacksmith—who cares for the horse's feet, and medical and dental care. If you do not have enough land or a safe barn or stable to keep a horse, you will need to pay to keep it in a boarding stable, where workers will feed and care for your horse.

*Horses are great pets, but they require a lot of space, time, money, and patience. You must be sure you can properly care for a horse before you decide to get one.*

## Do You Have Space for a Horse?

If you live on a farm, ranch, or in a country area where your family owns a large field to use as a fenced-in, grassy pasture, you might have enough space to keep your horse. But you need to make sure the pasture is safe, and that your horse has shelter there. If your family has other horses, your horse might be able to share the pasture with them.

Some cities and towns allow you to keep a horse on your property. There are specific laws about this, so you must have an adult find out about the rules. Some cities may allow you to keep one horse, but you must have at least

*Horses need a lot of space. Even smaller horses should have an enclosed field or pasture where they can run and play.*

2.5 acres of pasture for it to graze in. The adult should also check with an insurance company—a business that helps protect you, your horse, and your property—to see what their rules are.

## Finding a Stable

If you cannot keep your horse on your own property, you need to find and pay for a stable that will shelter and care for it. This stable should also have

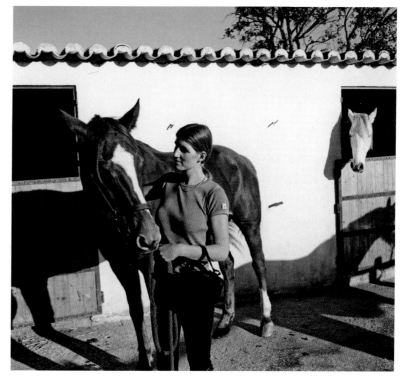

*Always carefully examine a stable before choosing one for your horse. Make sure it looks clean and that the people working there take good care of the horses.*

fenced-in pastures or areas where your horse can walk or run freely. A horse should not be kept in a stable all day and all night. The best way to find a good stable is to visit several stables and talk to their owners. Also talk to a riding instructor or another person who knows what horses need. Some stables have instructors who can help you learn how to care for a horse. Spend time there watching and learning, and ask a lot of questions. Doing a lot of research can help you with this process.

*As with all pets, you will need to spend a lot of time making sure your horse is happy and healthy. This includes feeding it, grooming it, and cleaning up after it.*

## Do You Have Time for a Horse?

Like all pets, a horse is a living creature that needs constant care. If you decide to get a horse, you must be sure you really want to take care of it. Horses can live for many years and getting one means you are responsible for caring for it throughout its life. You must be sure that you can do this before getting a horse as a pet.

Horses require a lot of your time every day. Besides needing food and water, a horse that lives in a stable needs to exercise at least twice a day. If you

*Even when the weather is cold, you must take the time to make sure your horse is happy and healthy.*

cannot do this yourself, you must be sure the stable has workers who will exercise your horse for you and make sure that the horse has enough food and water.

Horses are herd animals—they like to be with others. They need constant companionship and sights and activities that will spark their interest. In the wild, they would get both from other horses in their herd. This means that you will need to spend a lot of time with your horse—petting it, grooming it, talking to it, and riding it. You will also need time each day to make sure your horse is healthy.

If you are going to take care of its stall—its own "room" in the stable— you will find it takes time and hard work to keep the stall clean. You will need to spend time bringing in fresh hay, food, and water. But your reward will be a healthy, happy, and trusting companion.

# 3

# Choosing Your Horse

**O**nce you and your family decide to make a horse a part of your family, you must make many other decisions. The horse you choose should be the right size and **breed,** or type, for your property or for the stable where you will keep it.

What kind of horse should you get? There are many different kinds of horses. Should it be a young horse, or an older horse? If you want a horse just for pleasure riding, an older horse—but one that is not too old—that is used to riding on trails may be the right horse for you. Older horses with experience on trails will be less likely to be scared by sudden noises or movement.

Many people who are experienced with horses say that a child's horse should be between at least five and ten years old. Questions to ask when choosing a horse for a child include: Is the horse calm and good with children? Does it have a kind, patient nature? Many recommend a Quarter Horse

*Choosing the right horse is an important process that includes doing research, asking questions, and visiting with different types of horses.*

*If you plan on riding your horse, you must make sure to choose one that is used to riders and is the right size for you.*

for a child's first horse because of its sweet, gentle nature. To be on the safe side, you should choose a horse that has been ridden by children before. You should also learn to ride before you get a horse. This will make you more comfortable around your new pet. Also, if you take riding lessons at a stable, you can learn a lot about how to take care of your horse.

## Horse Breeds

There are more than 150 breeds of horses. Different breeds are divided into four main groups: light horses, heavy horses, ponies, and miniature horses. Horses come in many colors. Palominos have golden coats, with white manes and tails. Different shades of brown have many different names: bay, roan, and chestnut, for example. Horses can be all black or dappled grey, which is a grey coat with darker gray rings. Some have coats of two colors—some, like the raindrop horses, are spotted. Others, such as paint, or pinto horses, look like their coats have been splashed with paint.

Horses have a variety of markings, too. A horse's face may have a blaze, or a streak of white running from above the eyes down to its muzzle. Some can have a star, which is a white spot between the eyes. Its feet and legs may have markings called socks or stockings. Remember, though, that no matter how pretty a horse is, it is still the horse's nature that is most important.

## Light Horses

With their small bones and thin legs, light horses were developed for speed. Today they are popular as saddle horses for riding, racing, and show jumping. Some of these horses include the Arabian, Thoroughbred, Quarter Horse, and the Tennessee Walking Horse.

### ARABIANS

Many people think the Arabian horse is the most beautiful in the world. It is thought to be the oldest and purest breed, and valued greatly for its intelligence, strength, and its character. Ancient pictures of horses that look like Arabians are clues to this breed's long history. The pictures show that these horses may have lived in Arab—or Middle Eastern—lands thousands of years ago. Arabian horses have small heads and short backs. They have seventeen ribs—other horses have eighteen—and fewer bones in their backs and tail

*Many people like to have Arabian horses because of the graceful way that the horses move.*

than other horses do. They are between 14.2 and 15 **hands** (more than 4 feet to 5 feet) tall. Their tails, manes, and coats are of silky hair. Most Arabians are white or gray, but they can be other colors.

## THOROUGHBREDS

In the third century, Arabians and other horses called Barbs were brought to England. Barbs came from the coasts of Morocco, Tunisia, and Algeria. Together, these areas were called the Barbary Coast. Like the Arabians, the Barbs had boundless energy and great speed. Interest in horse racing was growing in England and in other European countries. Before long, **breeders** mixed the Arabians with the Barbs, which are mostly gray, bay (reddish brown, with black on its mane, tail, lower legs, and edges of its ears), brown, or black. The Thoroughbred, which was born to run, was developed from these breeds.

## QUARTER HORSES

The ancestors of the Quarter Horse go back to the horses brought to America by the Spanish explorers and a stallion named Janus. Janus was a small Thoroughbred stallion brought to Virginia in the late 1700s. English settlers bred quarter horses to be their workhorses for farmwork and for pulling carriages or wagons. Quarter Horses were great at herding cattle, especially "cutting," or sorting out, certain cows from the herd. These horses could sense what a cow's next move was going to be and prevent that by stopping and turning while galloping at top speed.

Settlers began racing their speedy horses for distances of a quarter of a mile, which is how the horses got their name. As machines replaced horses on ranches and farms, the Quarter Horse became a popular riding horse. Quarter Horses are used in the sport of polo because they can start, stop, and turn so quickly. Quarter Horses can be any color, and they be around 14 to 16 hands (about 4 to 5 feet) tall.

*Quarter Horses can be a variety of colors.*

## TENNESSEE WALKING HORSES

Americans have developed some kinds of horses that have special **gaits,** or ways of moving, that no other horse has. The Tennessee Walking Horse has three gaits—flat-foot walk, the running walk (with its long, fast stride), and the canter, which is a fast, three-beat gait with a rocking-horse motion. Southern plantation workers rode these horses as they traveled long distances around their fields to inspect the crops. These horses' sweet nature makes them a fine choice for beginning riders. Tennessee Walkers average 15.2 hands (about 5 feet tall) and come in several colors.

*The first Tennessee Walking Horses were bred in the United States, from a combination of different horse breeds*

## Draft Horses

Heavy horses are the tallest, heaviest, and strongest breeds. Called draft horses, these breeds were developed for hard work, hauling all sorts of heavy loads. Among these breeds are the Shire, Clydesdale, Percheron, and Belgian Draft horses.

*Shires and other draft horses are very large and strong. This is why they were most often used for pulling heavy loads and difficult farmwork.*

## SHIRES

These huge horses stand from 16 to more than 19 hands (about 5 to more than 6 feet) tall. They are an English breed, descended from the "Great Horse" of medieval times. Medieval horses were very big and strong. They had to be, since they wore armor and carried armored knights into battle. As years passed, Shires became part of everyday life in England and were brought to North and South America, Russia, and Australia. These powerful yet gentle giants are fine workers on farms and haul heavy loads in cities.

## CLYDESDALES

The Clydesdale was developed in Scotland to meet the needs of both farmers and merchants. They stand from 16 to 17 hands (between 5 and 6 feet) tall and are bay, brown, or black. These horses have big ears and bright eyes. They usually have white blazes and stockings, with a generous amount of white hair, called feathers, around their feet. Clydesdales are often used on farms and in forests. These magnificent horses also compete in horse shows and march in parades.

## PERCHERONS

Percherons originally came from an ancient part of France called La Perche. Their ancestors were Arabian horse. Percherons are usually from 15 to 17 hands (between 5 and 6 feet tall), although one Percheron named Dr. Le Gear grew to be 21 hands (7 feet) at his **withers**—the ridge between his shoulders where the bones of his neck and back joined. The people who first developed and raised Percheron horses gave

*A group of black Percherons runs through their pasture.*

them much attention and affection. Percherons, like Shires, are powerful yet gentle partners. At first they pulled coaches that carried people. When railways were built, Percherons pulled the cars along the tracks. Percherons were so strong that they replaced oxen on farms. Even bigger Percherons were bred to pull heavy loads from trading ships docked in harbors and from trains.

## Ponies

Ponies are less than 14.2 hands (about 4.8 feet) tall. They come from all over the world, most from places with cold, stormy climates. Some come from

*Pony breeds, such as this Shetland pony, do not grow to be very large, but they still need the same kind of care as larger horses.*

mountainous countries, and others from flat, rocky lands or islands. Not much grass and very few plants grow in these places, so ponies do not eat a lot of grass. But they are tough and very strong. They are high-spirited, and some can be stubborn at times. Their bodies are wide, and their legs are short. Their manes and tails are thicker and longer than those of larger horses.

*Connemara ponies are excellent for riding and jumping.*

## SHETLANDS

Shetland ponies come from the Shetland Islands far north and east of Scotland, near the Arctic Circle. Shetlands have thick, long manes and grow double coats that keep them warm in the cold climate. They are one of the strongest animals for their size. Some Shetlands can pull loads as heavy as those pulled by big draft horses. Shetlands are very smart, but can be very stubborn, too. Miners once used Shetlands in the narrow tunnels of coal mines because the horses were small and could pull carts loaded with coal up from the mines. Today Shetland ponies are popular pets and are often used as therapy horses or for children's events.

## CONNEMARAS

Many people think that Connemara ponies are the best show jumpers and riding ponies. They come from Ireland's rocky western coast, and have been bred there for many centuries. Most are gray, but others can be brown, black, chestnut, roan, or other colors.

## Miniature Horses

Miniature horses are smaller than ponies, but resemble larger horses. These beautiful little horses stand no more than 34 inches tall at the withers. Because of their size, they are not for riding. But many owners have their horses compete in different types of shows. The American Miniature Horse Youth Association for children is one group that sponsors many miniature horse shows. Miniature horses are not just for children. Many adults also participate in clubs, show their horses, and enjoy their companionship.

*Miniature horses are often entered in shows and competitions. They are also very popular with families who love horses but cannot have larger ones.*

## Where To Find a Horse

If you and your family are about to buy your first horse, the first step should be to talk to your riding instructor or others you know who are knowledgeable about horses. They can point you toward the best places and ways to buy horses. There are many different places where you will find horses for sale.

The Internet is one place, and classified ads in newspapers and horse publications are others. Bulletin boards in feed stores or tack (horse supply) shops may have flyers listing horses for sale. You must be very careful about whom and where you buy from. Whenever you go to look at horses for sale, bring along your riding instructor or another person who knows horses well. Public sales and horse auctions are not always the best places to find the right horse. Things happen fast at a public sale, and you may not get time to really look at the horse you like. If you plan on riding your horse, you should be able to test-ride it and handle it.

If you are looking at horses offered for sale by a horse dealer, you will probably have time to watch them being handled and to ride them. Some dealers may let you try the horse out at home. You can also buy your horse from a private home that has advertised a horse for sale, but you must be careful. Be sure to ask how long they have had the horse and why it is for sale.

*You must make sure that you will be able to handle and care for the horse you choose.*

Make a checklist so you will not forget any questions that you want to ask. You should ask lot of questions about how the horse behaves in different situations—when it is put into its stall, for example. Look for kick marks in the stall, and signs of chewing. These could be signs that the horse is unhappy about being kept in a stall or is difficult when being placed there.

When you find the horse you want, before you buy it, have a **veterinarian,** called a vet for short, examine it. If the person selling the horse has nothing to hide, he or she will not mind having your vet check it. You and your family should be there so that you can talk with the vet as the horse is examined. In most cases, the vet will give you an official paper called a certificate. The certificate lists facts

*Carefully choosing the right type of horse or pony can lead to many happy years with a new friend.*

about the horse and has the doctor's report. It also says if the horse is right for your purpose, whether it is for pleasure riding or for competing in horse shows.

Choosing the right horse is a very important step toward owning a horse. You should take your time, explore all options available to you, and make a careful decision.

## ADOPTION

Many local horse clubs, animal shelters, or farms will advertise horses that are up for adoption. Some of these horses have been rescued, or taken from bad situations or unfit homes, and are need of good homes with kind owners. Other adoptable horses sometimes come from families that can no longer afford to keep the horse or do not have enough space for it.

When you apply to adopt a horse, the organization that is in charge will interview you and check where you will be keeping the horse. They do this to make sure that you and the horse will be a good fit. Most of the time, a fee or donation to the organization is required before you can have the horse. Be sure to ask your own questions. Ask why the horse is up for adoption, how old it is, and does it like or dislike children or dogs, cats, and other animals. Also be sure to have a vet check its health. Many people are happy with adopted horses, but they might not be the right choice for everyone. Do your research and think carefully before deciding to rescue or adopt a horse.

# 4

# Life with Your Horse

Whether your horse lives in a pasture with a shelter or in a stable, taking care of it takes a lot of time and work. If the horse is kept in a stable, you must make sure that the horse has enough space. Your horse should not have enough space to run around in the stable, but it should have enough room in its stall to move a bit and lie down. Adult horses most often rest while standing. However, a horse will lie down for a short rest each day if it has a nice, roomy place to do so. The bedding where it rests needs to be clean and dry. This means periodically shoveling out the horse poop and dirty hay and replacing it with clean hay.

Horses that live in pastures should have some form of shelter they can go to when the weather is bad or when they want to go indoors. Horses that run free in the wild will go under trees or near rocks to protect themselves from wind and weather. But horses in pastures or in

*This horse and his friend won first place in a local horse show. Horses are good workers and great show animals, but most importantly, they are excellent companions.*

*The door of your horse's stall should have a simple lock to prevent the horse from escaping.*

**paddocks** need wooden shelters for protection. The shelters should be large enough to contain all the horses that graze together, since they like to be in each other's company, and should be large enough to prevent overcrowding. The roof must be high enough to provide plenty of room for the horses' heads. The roof should be sloping so that rain or snow will run off. The safest shelters are open in front, so that a horse can run from any dangers or other horses. Fixtures for storing hay, other feed, or equipment should be high off the ground, to prevent injuries. Some small shelters may have doors, which are helpful if horses or ponies need to be kept inside from time to time.

When your horse is outside, make sure the fences around the pasture are strong. Never use barbed wire, which has sharp metal parts that can hurt the horse, and be sure there are no nails sticking out of the fence. The boards of the fence should be close together so your horse will not get its head stuck between them. Fences should be at least 5 feet high so your horse will not jump over it. Gates should open into the pasture so your horse cannot push them open and run out. Also watch for things like buckets or pitchforks lying around in the barn, stable, or pasture shelter since they could cause accidents.

## Drinking and Eating

Horses drink five to twenty-five gallons of water a day, so fresh water should always be there for them. Horses in paddocks or at pasture may have a natural stream or river nearby, but it is possible that this source may be polluted. If it is not, the horses can drink from it, as long as there is gravel at the bottom. If sand is at the bottom of the stream or river, the horses could swallow sand together with the water. You

*Most horses drink from troughs that are cleaned and refilled regularly.*

# DANGER!

As with all animals, there are certain things that horses should not eat. Some are just unhealthy for them, such as human foods and table scraps. There are also many plants, shrubs, and trees that are poisonous to horses. You must be sure never to feed your horse these things. If your horse grazes in a pasture, you must make sure there are no poisonous plants, shrubs, or trees. Winds may blow plant seeds or parts into the pasture, so you need to check the pasture every week to make sure no new poisonous plants are growing. For example, eating any part of a yew tree, whether the tree is dead or alive, can kill a horse. If some trees or shrubs cannot be removed, then you must fence them off so your horse cannot reach them. When riding your horse along a trail or letting it graze in a field, make sure it does not eat any plants that you are not familiar with. If you think your horse may have eaten a poisonous plant contact your vet immediately. For horses, yew and ragwort plants are the most deadly, but here are other plants that can cause sickness, pain, or even death:

- acorns
- bracken
- buttercup
- flax
- foxglove
- goldenchain tree
- hemlock
- horsetail plant
- laurel
- monkshood
- nightshade
- oak
- oleander
- potato plant
- privet
- rhododendron
- sorghum
- St. John's Wort

must make sure that the ground that leads to the stream or river is clean and relatively flat. A riverbank that has a steep slope is dangerous—the horse could slide down it, and the bank could eventually collapse.

To provide fresh, clean water, many horse owners use a special metal trough, which is a large metal container that does not rust easily. Some troughs are automatically filled with water from pipes buried deep underground. This is a good alternative to a clean, running stream. Most other troughs are not automatic, and are filled by pouring buckets of water. The water in those troughs cannot be left there for long—it must be dumped out daily and the troughs must be thoroughly cleaned and refilled. Smaller containers such as buckets may be used to provide water, but these could be overturned. A bucket placed in the center of an old, used tire set on the ground would be less likely to be knocked over.

A horse that lives in a stable may drink from about 5 to 10 gallons of water a day. You will need a heavy-duty rubber water bucket for a stabled horse. Rubber is safer than plastic, and metal buckets are dangerous since they can cause injuries to a horse that is moving around in its stall. Keep buckets in a corner of the stable, not near the door, but not too far from it, so they are easy to refill. A bucket can be fixed to the wall with clips so that your horse will not kick it over or step in or on it.

Never give your horse water while it is moving around and then let it stand stil—your horse could get sick. Keep your horse moving after it drinks. If you are out trail riding and he gets hot, give your horse all the water it wants, as long as you keep riding or walking

*It is natural for horses to graze on the plants available in their frields or pastures. But it is important to keep an eye out for plants that could be poisonous.*

Your horse needs two kinds of feed (horse food is called feed): **roughage,** or forage, such as pasture grass or hay, and grain. Other kinds of feed include oats, alfalfa, soybeans, clover, and other plants. Sweet feed that contains molasses and other sugars such as beet pulp or citrus pulp, and pelleted feeds can also be fed. Ask your vet how much to feed your horse, and what kind of diet is best. You can find feed shops advertised online, in horse magazines and newsletters, or in newspapers or the phone book. Many horse tack shops that sell riding equipment, such as saddles, bridles and other riding gear, also sell horse feed.

Since a horse's instinct is to graze, you can schedule feedings two or three times a day, rather than letting it gobble it all up at once. Of course, horses like treats, too, especially red apples and carrots. The apples and carrots should be cut in small pieces.

## Handling Your Horse

Before you even get a horse, you must make sure you are comfortable handling it. This means touching it and grooming it. If you plan on riding the horse, you must be comfortable with putting on its saddle and bridle and riding it. If you have never owned a horse before, it is important to take riding lessons or join a club that teaches you how to ride and care for a horse. Once you have your horse, do not handle it, groom it, or ride it without adult supervision. This is to make sure that you and your horse stay safe!

*Besides teaching you to ride, riding lessons can help you become more comfortable around horses and show you how to take care of your new friend.*

## Grooming

Your horse will need to be groomed daily. Some of the grooming supplies you will need include sponges, cloths, and brushes, a comb for grooming, and a hoof pick. Give your horse a quick grooming before you ride. Sponge off any stable stains such as dried urine and brush out any pieces of bedding caught in the mane or tail. Dirt under the saddle or bridle can cause saddle sores. After you ride, groom your horse again to keep it clean. With adult supervision,

*Keeping your horses's coat clean and smooth is important. Dirty or tangled coats that have insects or other pests can cause health problems for your horse.*

carefully check the hooves. Lift up a horse's hoof only if the horse is calm and if you and the horse are used to it. A kick from a nervous horse can be painful or even deadly! Pick out any pebbles or dirt and check its shoes to make sure they are not loose. Also look for cuts or sores. Every two months, have a farrier come to trim your horse's hoofs and attach new shoes.

## Exercise

If a horse can get exercise by running and chasing other

*Special tools are used to carefully pick out rocks and other harmful objects from your horse's hooves. Always use care whenever lifting your horse's feet.*

horses in a pasture, you will not need to exercise it as much. However, if your horse cannot do that, then you will need to ride your horse or exercise it in some other way for at least an hour or longer every day. If a horse is cooped up in a stable for hours and hours, it can develop some bad habits. These include biting the stall door or other objects nearby, pacing around and around in its stall, or swaying and weaving, with its head over the door.

*Horses of all sizes and ages need to be able to exercise to stay healthy.*

## Keeping Your Friend Healthy

You should have your horse checked at least once a year by a vet, who will examine him very thoroughly, from tail to teeth. Your horse must get special medication to prevent certain diseases. Also be on the lookout for signs that your horse is sick. Your horse may stop eating, limp, or paw at the ground. Sometimes horses lie down and will not get up. They can get colds, flu, or other illnesses, too. Horses can also have worms inside their bodies, especially if they are eating grass in a pasture. Your horse must be dewormed every six to eight weeks. Have a first-aid kit handy in case of an emergency. Talk to your vet about what to do in an emergency, and how to use items in the first-aid kit.

# Getting to Know Your Horse

What makes a horse happy? Horses enjoy the company of other horses. They communicate with each other, groom, and chase each other. If you have only one horse, try to find a way for it to be with others. You may have a friend who has horses and will let your horse share a pasture, barn, or stable. Make sure you watch the new horse until it gets used to being with the others. If there are no other horses, you will need to spend a lot of time grooming, riding, and talking to it.

*Most horses love tasty treats like carrots and apples.*

*With careful handling and proper care, you will be rewarded with many fun years with your horse.*

Your horse may be gentle, kind, and patient, and very willing to work with you. But it is important to learn the proper way to handle it. An experienced horse owner or instructor can help you. You can also learn by carefully watching your horse. Get to know your horse's normal moves and what they mean. What sounds does it make, and what do they mean? If a horse is scared, it will put its ears back, bare its teeth, and swish its tail. If it thinks it must protect itself, it will kick or bite. When a horse is suddenly frightened, it will run away as fast as it can. Knowing these signs can help you protect and handle your horse.

When you are training your horse, be gentle and patient. Your horse will learn from the tone of your voice whether you are happy with it or not. Most horses will be happy to learn the things you teach it.

Most horses enjoy pleasing their humans. With affection, trust, and understanding, you will have a magnificent companion for many years.

# Glossary

**breed**—A certain kind of horse, such as an Arabian or a Clydesdale.

**breeder**—A person who raises a certain kind of horse.

**farrier**—A blacksmith who makes steel horseshoes and nails them to a horse's hooves.

**gait**—A certain way of walking or running.

**hand**—The amount used to measure a horse's height. One hand equals about 4 inches.

**paddock**—A fenced-in field used as a pasture or a place to exercise a horse.

**roughage**—Grains and other kinds of feeds that help move food through a horse's stomach and intestines.

**tack**—Saddle, bridle, and other things you need to ride and control a horse.

**veterinarian**—A doctor who specializes in treating animals.

**withers**—The part of a horse between its shoulder bones. Hands are measured from the withers to the hooves.

# Find Out More

## Books

Clutton-Brock, Juliet. *Horse.* New York: DK Publishing, 2004.

Draper, Judith. *My First Horse and Pony Care Book.* Boston: Kingfisher, 2006.

Fetty, Margaret. *Show Horses.* New York: Bearport, 2007.

Jeffrey, Laura S. *Horses: How to Choose and Care for a Horse.* Berkeley Heights, NJ: Enslow Publishers, 2004.

Simon, Seymour. *Horses.* New York: HarperCollins Publishers, 2006.

## Web Sites

**American Miniature Horse Youth Association**
http://www.amha.org/index.asp?KeyName=710

**ASPCA: Horse Care**
http://www2.aspca.org/site/PageServer?pagename=pets_horsecare

**Choosing a Horse: Horse Breeds**
http://www.petpeoplesplace.com/resources/breed_profiles/horses

## For the First-time Horse Owner

http://equerry.com/html/ftho/eq_ftho.htm

## The Horse—The American Museum of Natural History

http://www.amnh.org/exhibitions/horse

## HORSEFUN

http://horsefun.com

## United States Humane Society General Horse Care Guidelines

http://www.hsus.org/horses_equines/companions/general_horse_care_guide-
  lines.html

## About the Author

Gail Mack grew up in Boston, Massachusetts, and learned to ride at camp when she was
ten years old. She rode there every summer for six years. Her favorite horse was Robin,
a friendly chestnut who always listened when she talked to him as they rode along.
Today, she lives in New York City and rides mostly subways and buses.

# Index

Page numbers for illustrations are in **bold.**